I0485439

HALLOWEEN COLORING BOOK

For Adults 2

Stress-Relieving Pumpkin Patterns

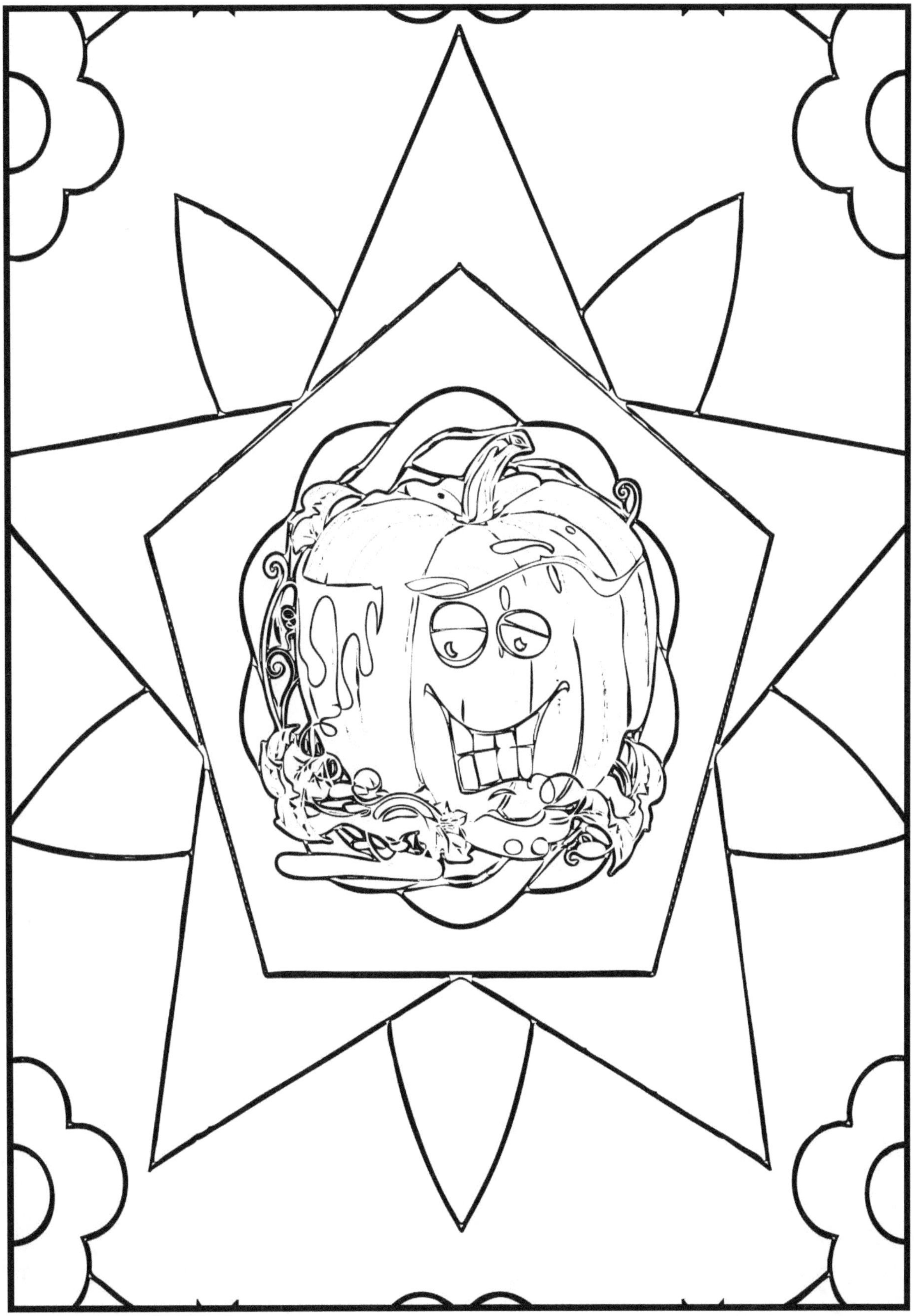

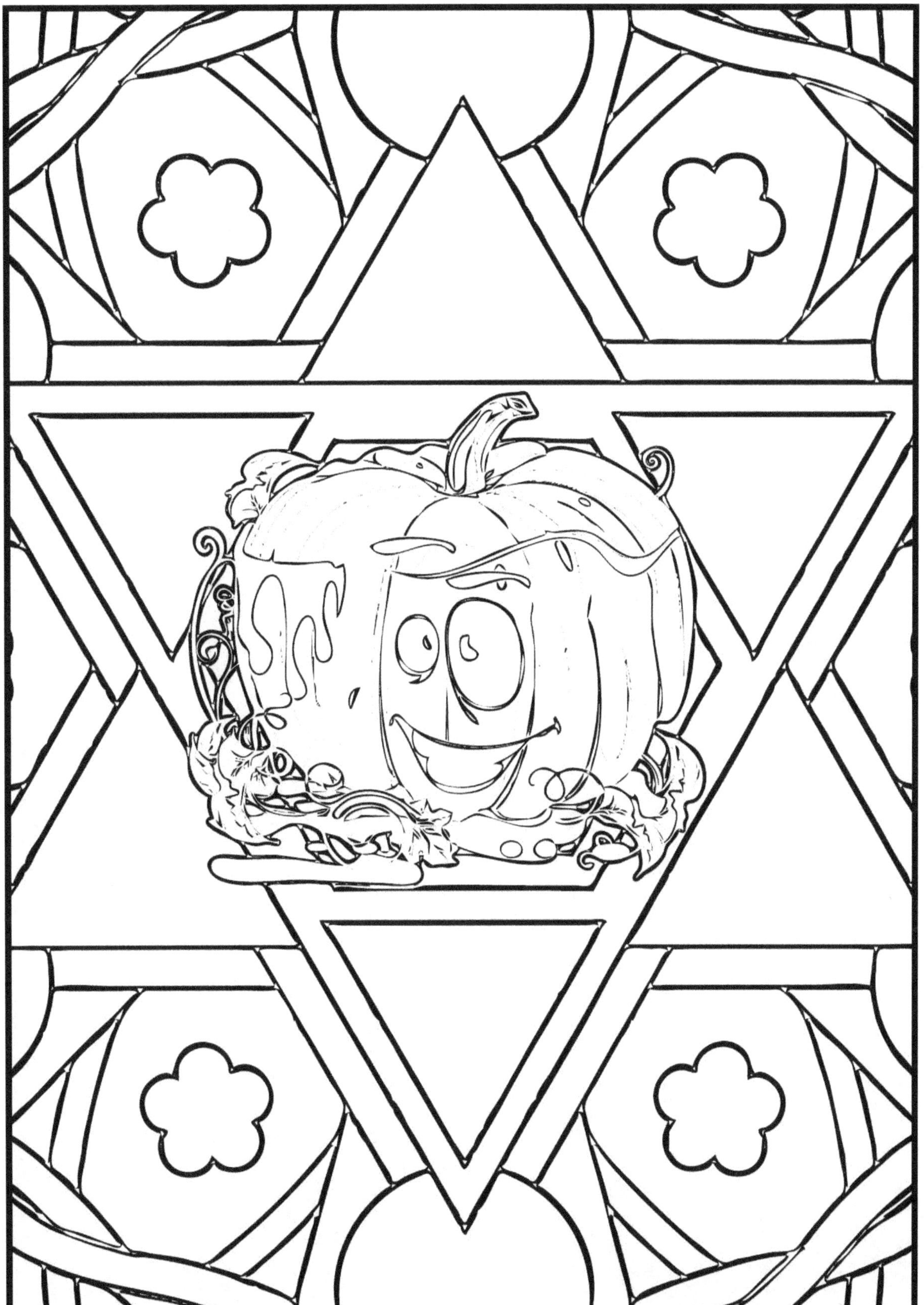

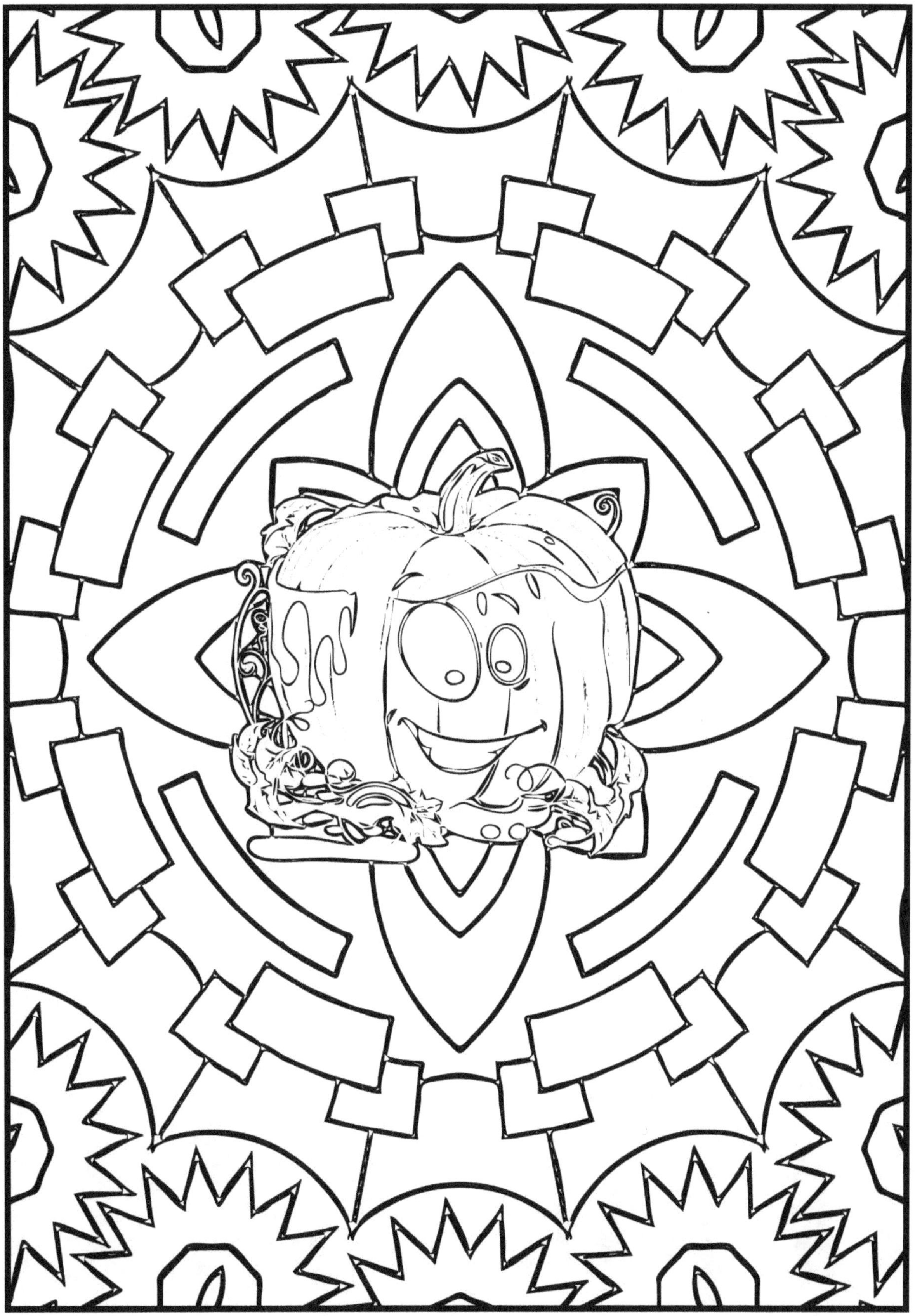

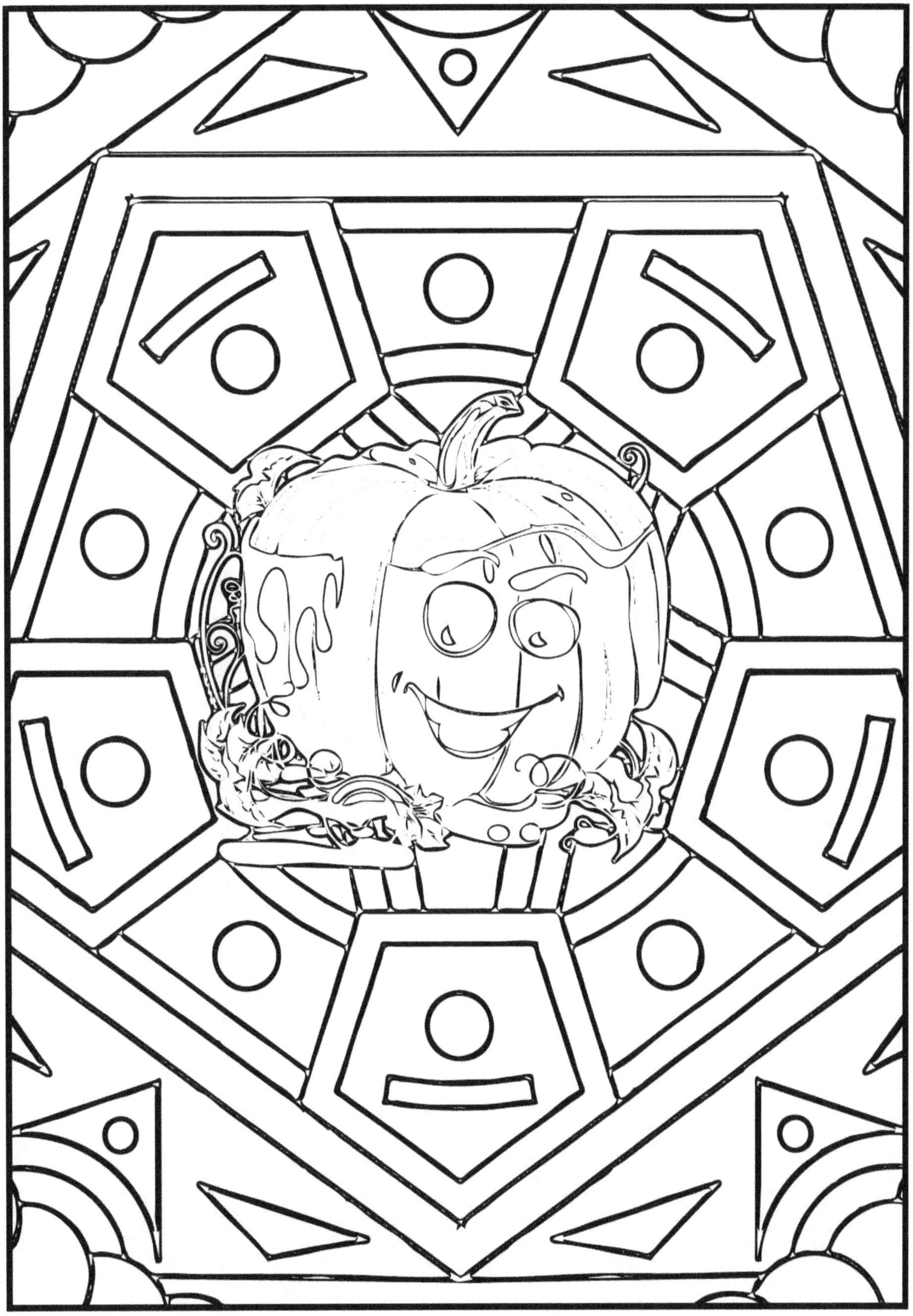

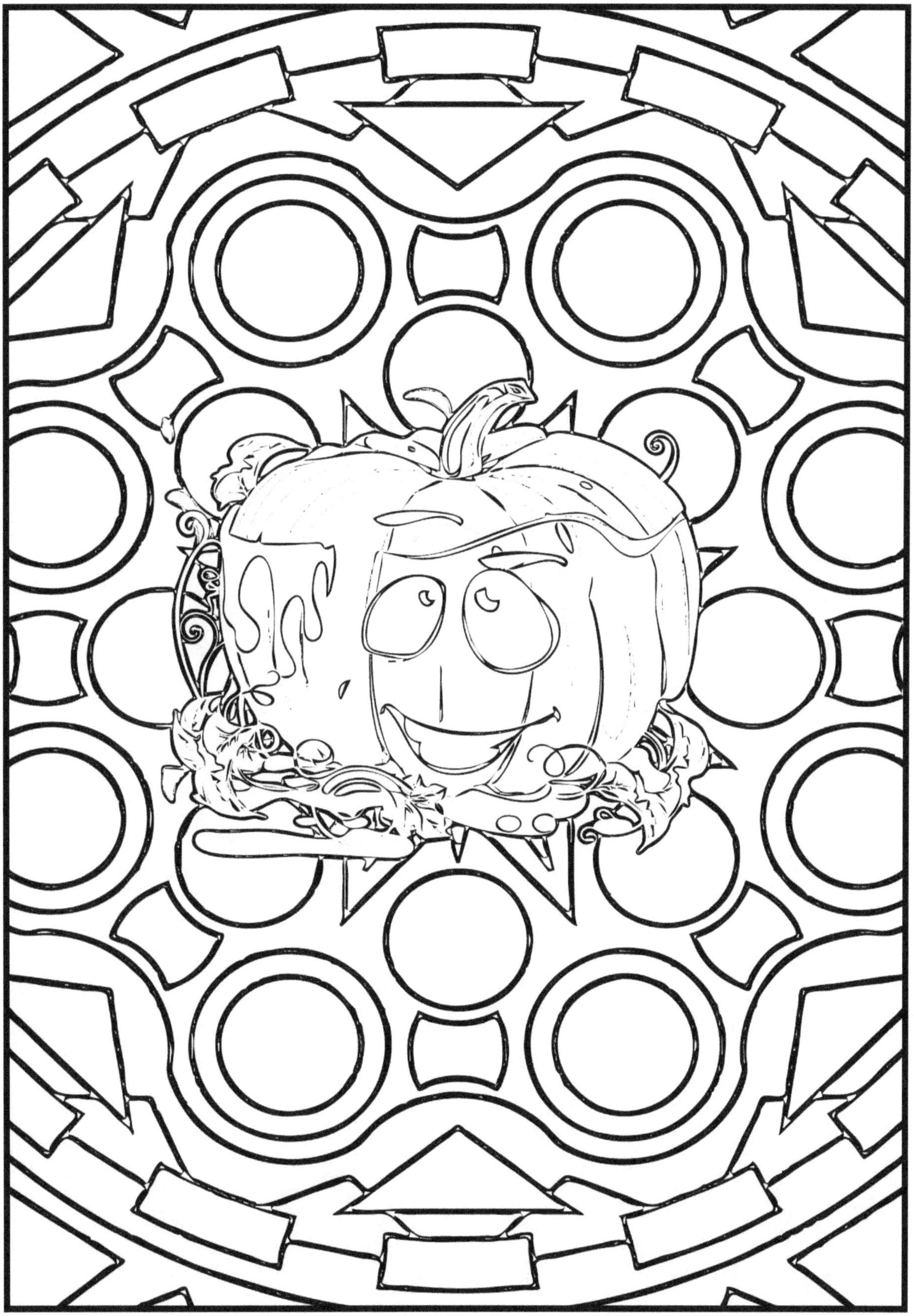

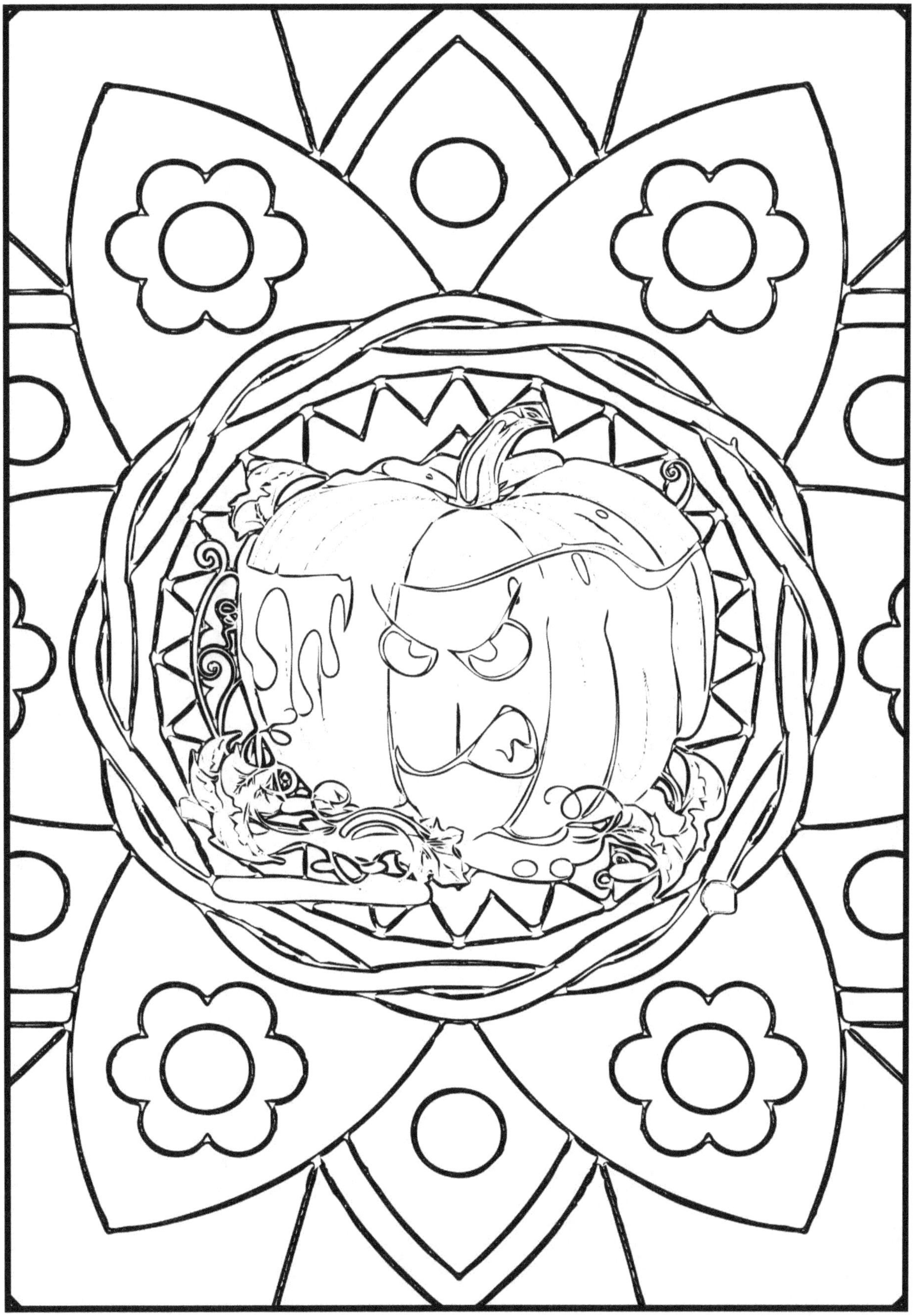

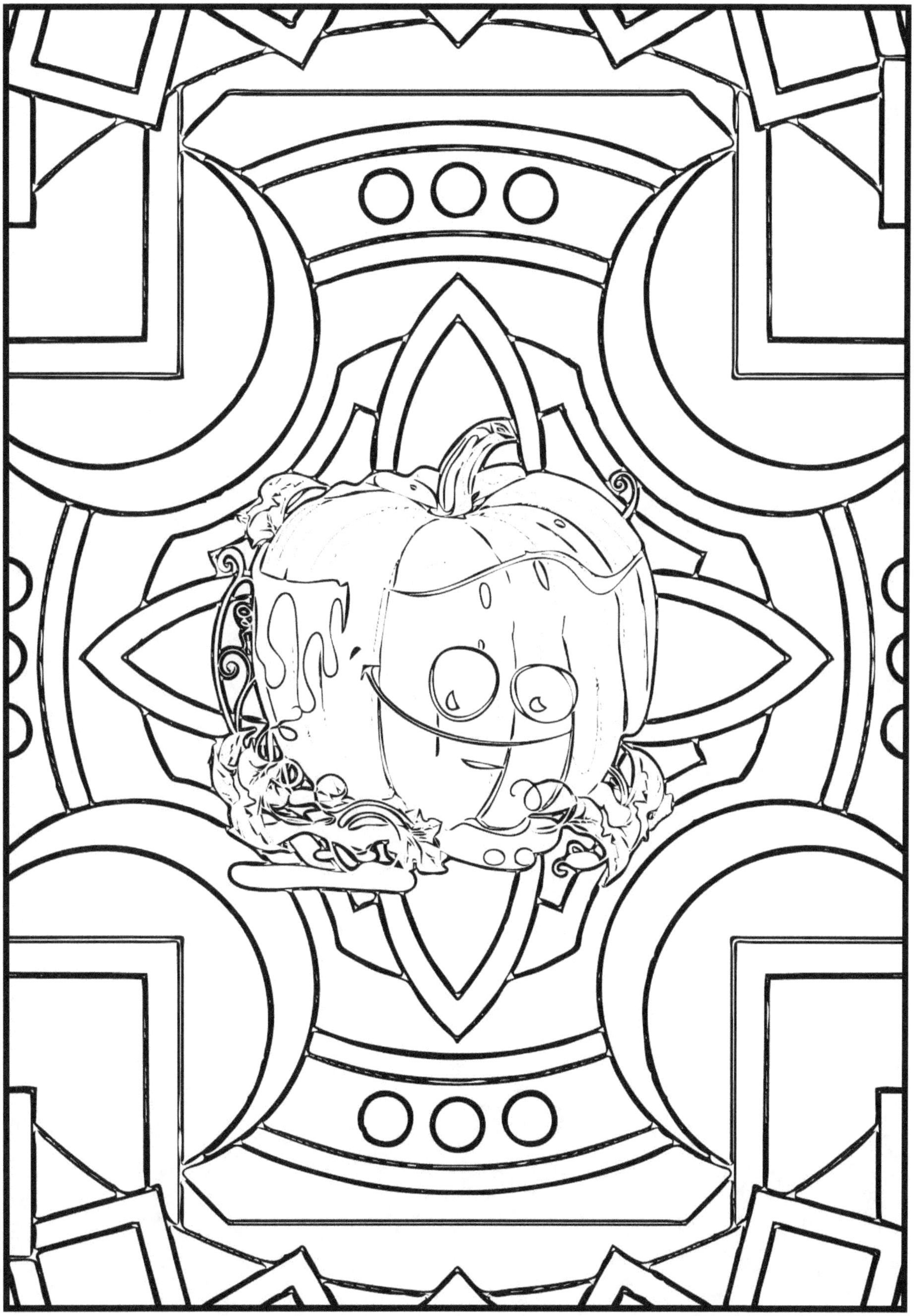

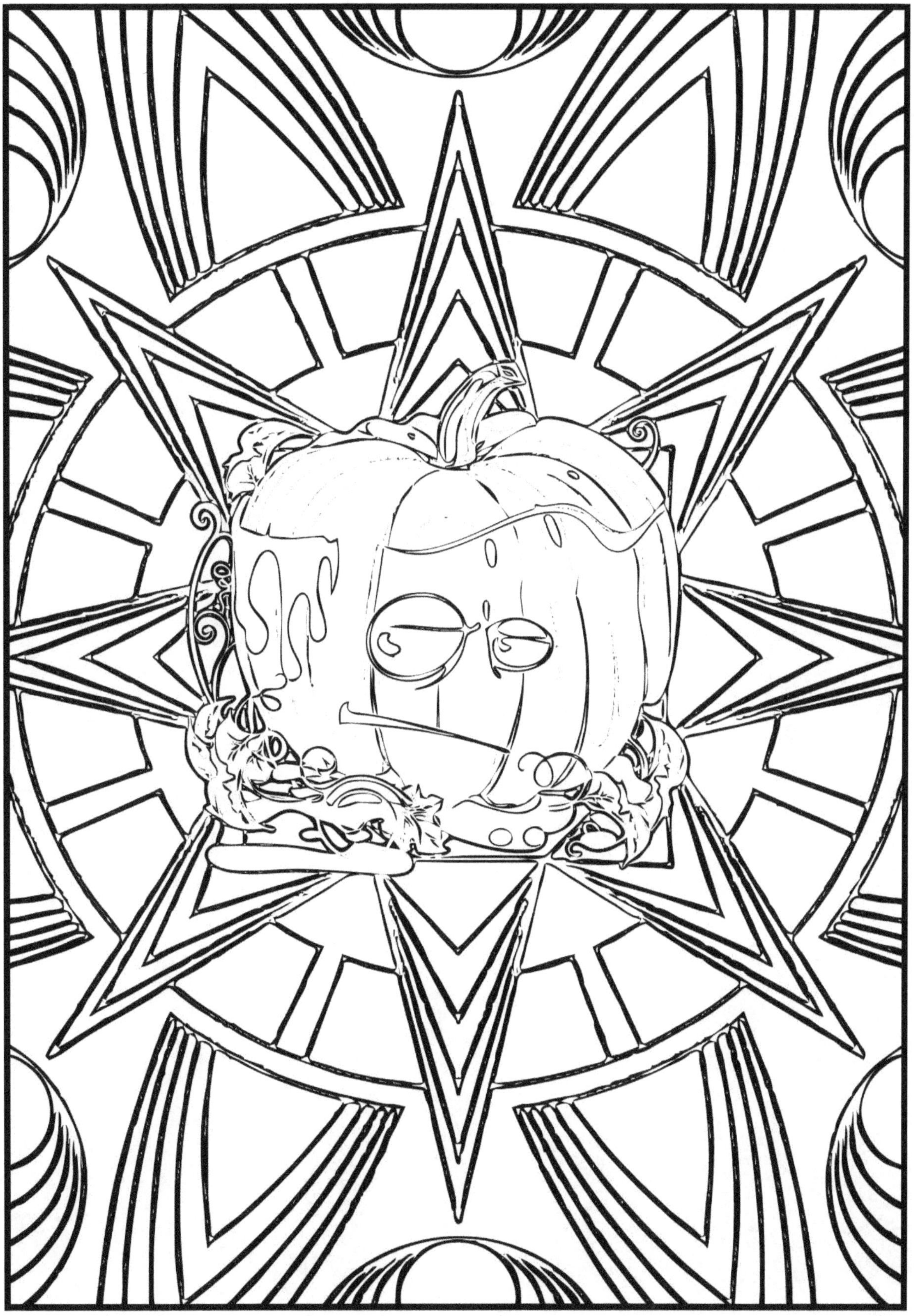

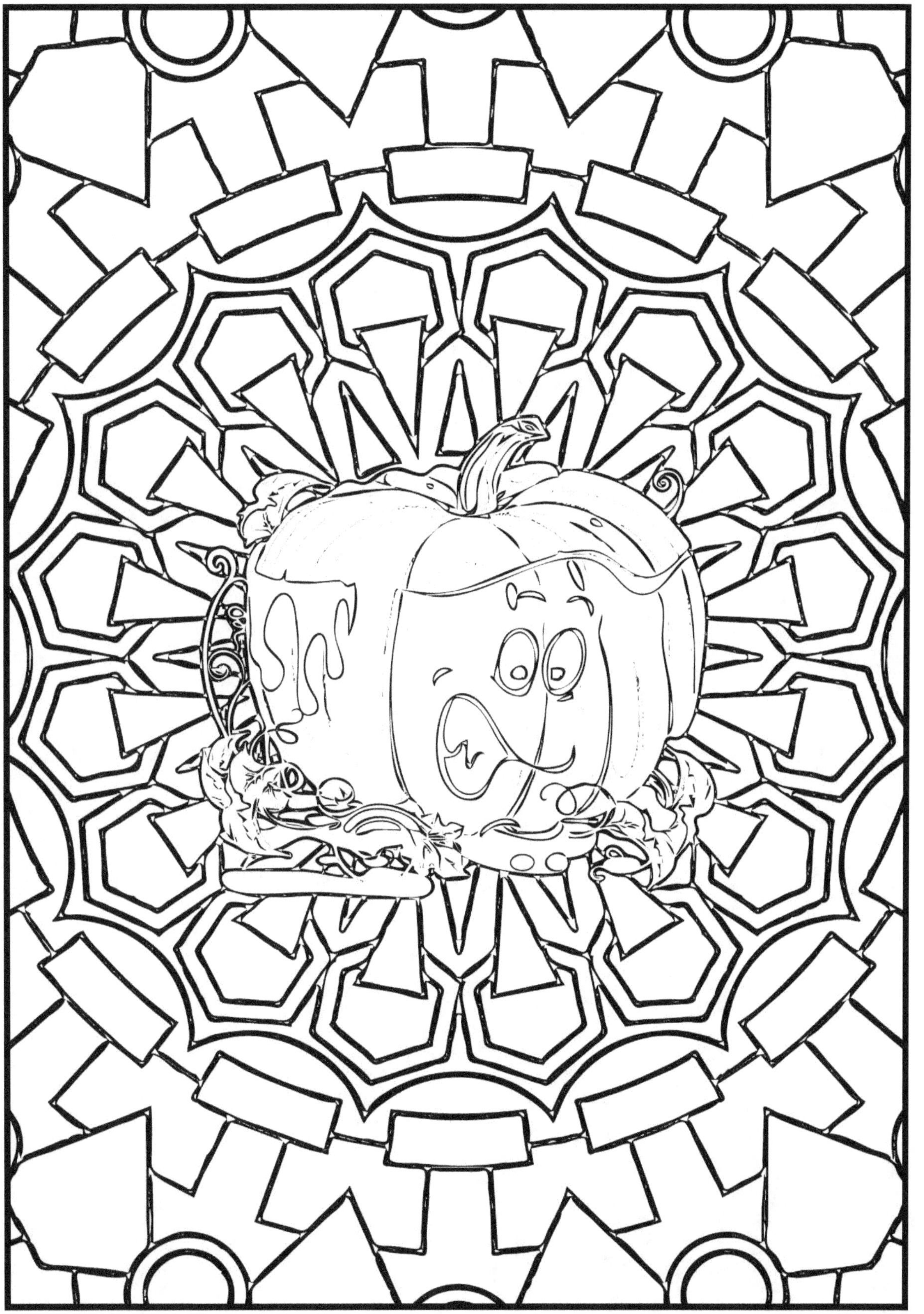

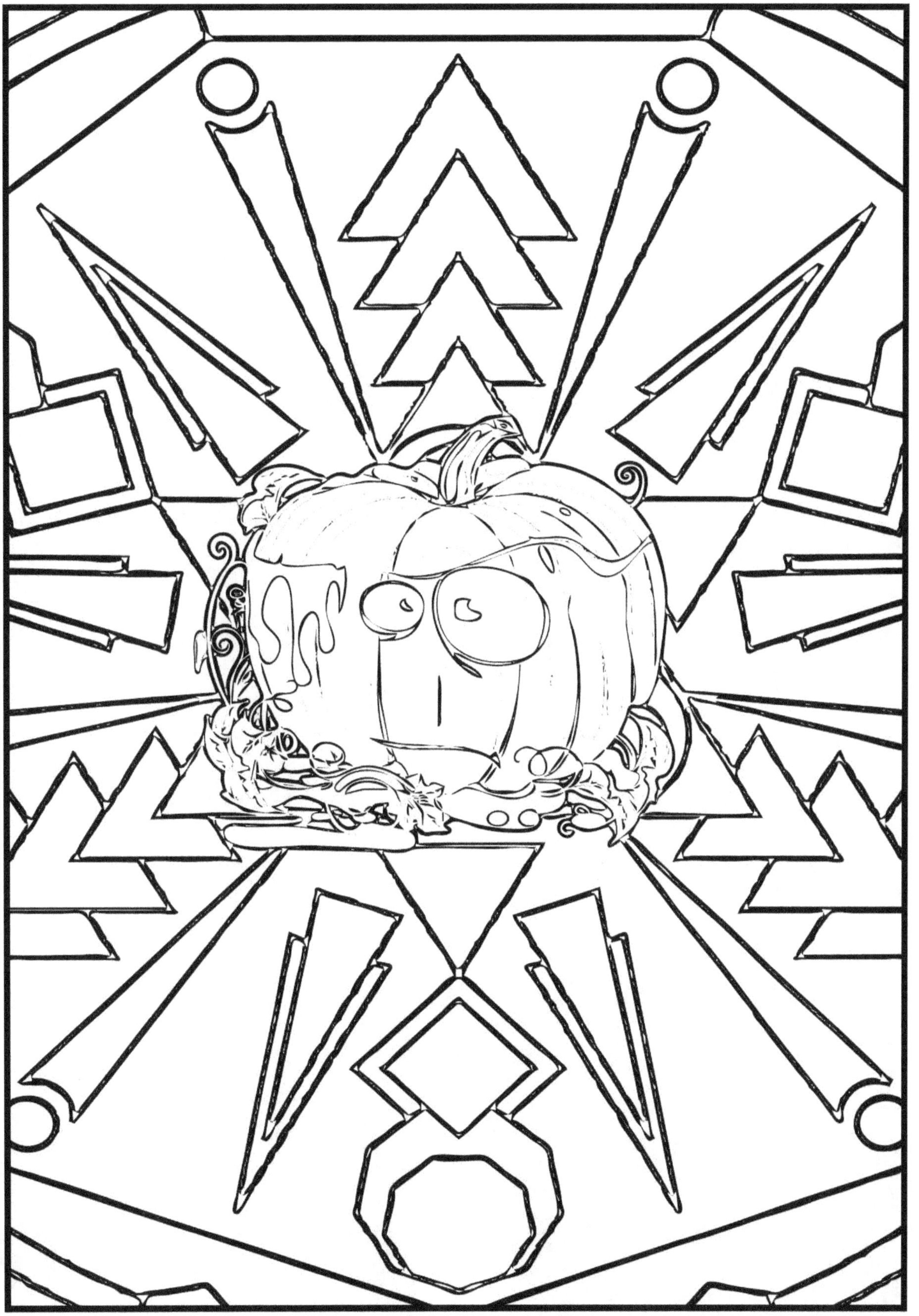

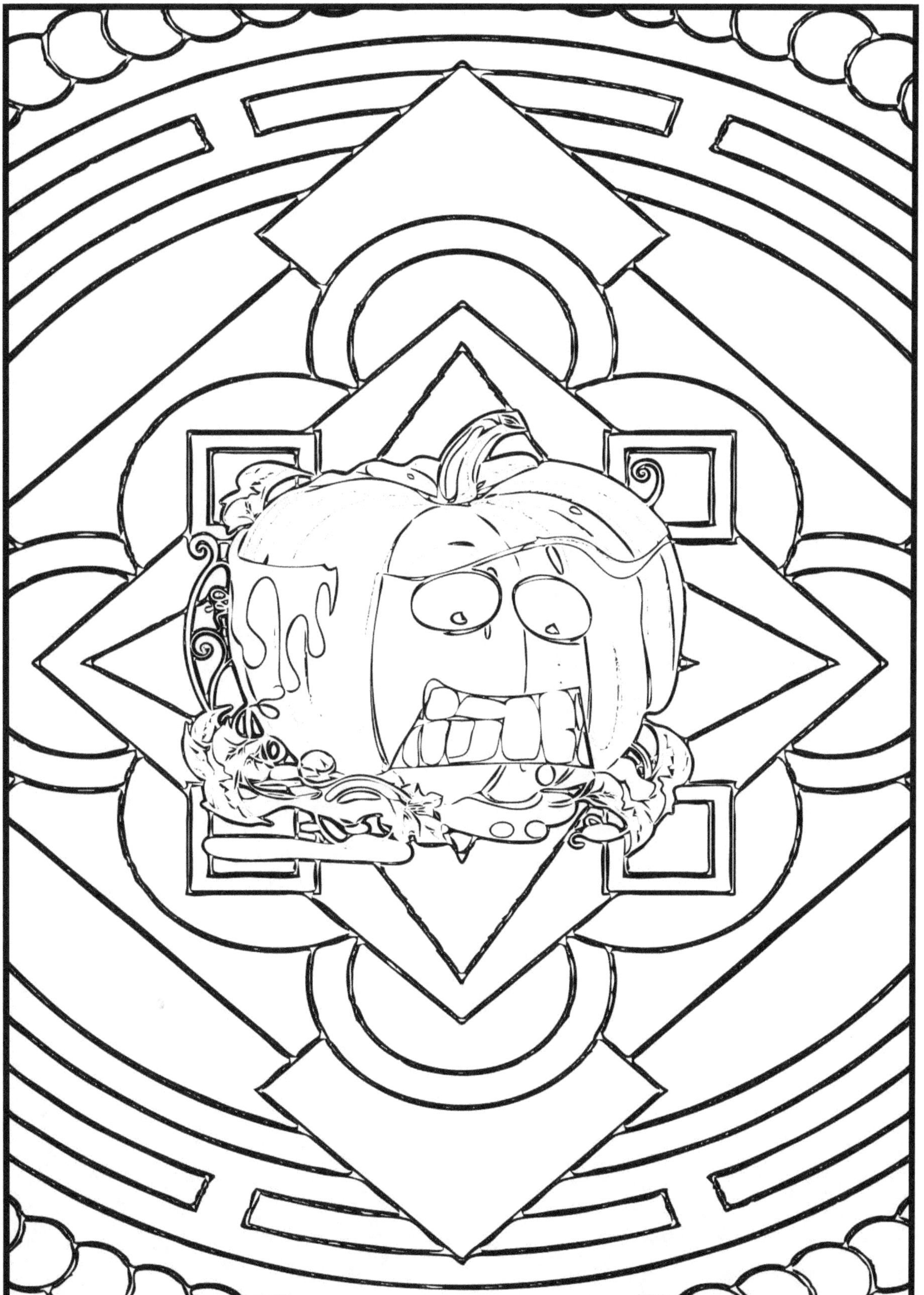

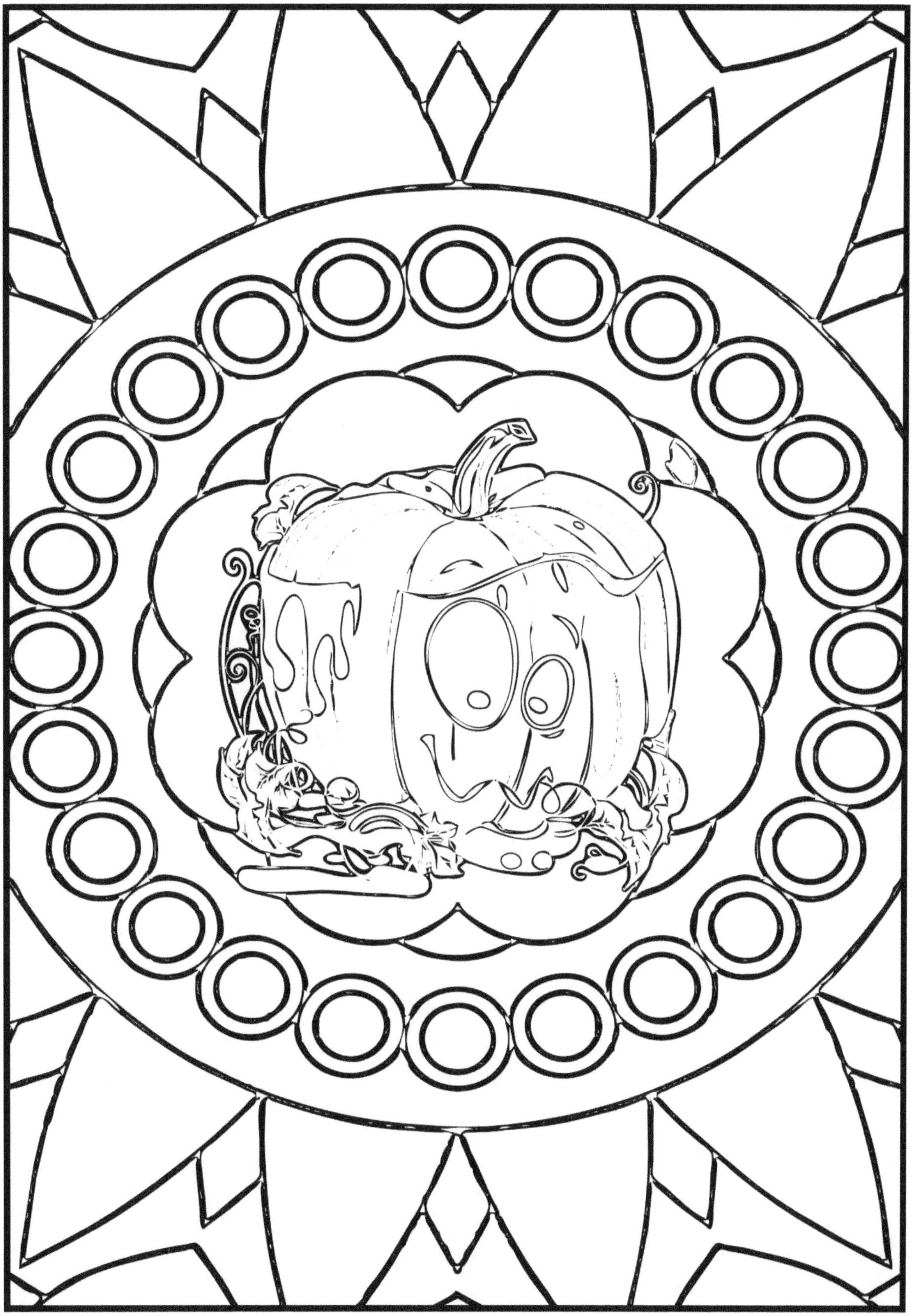

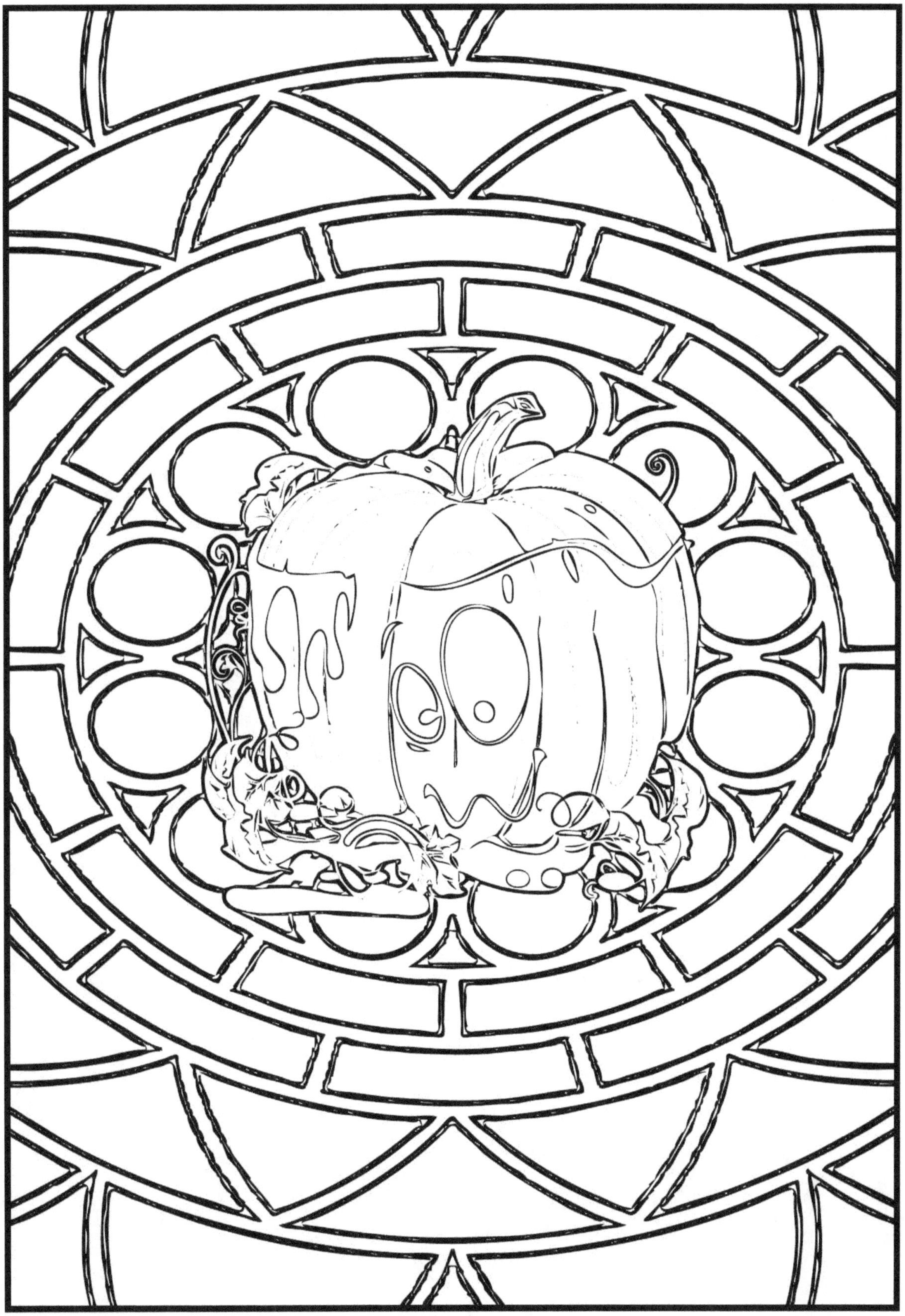

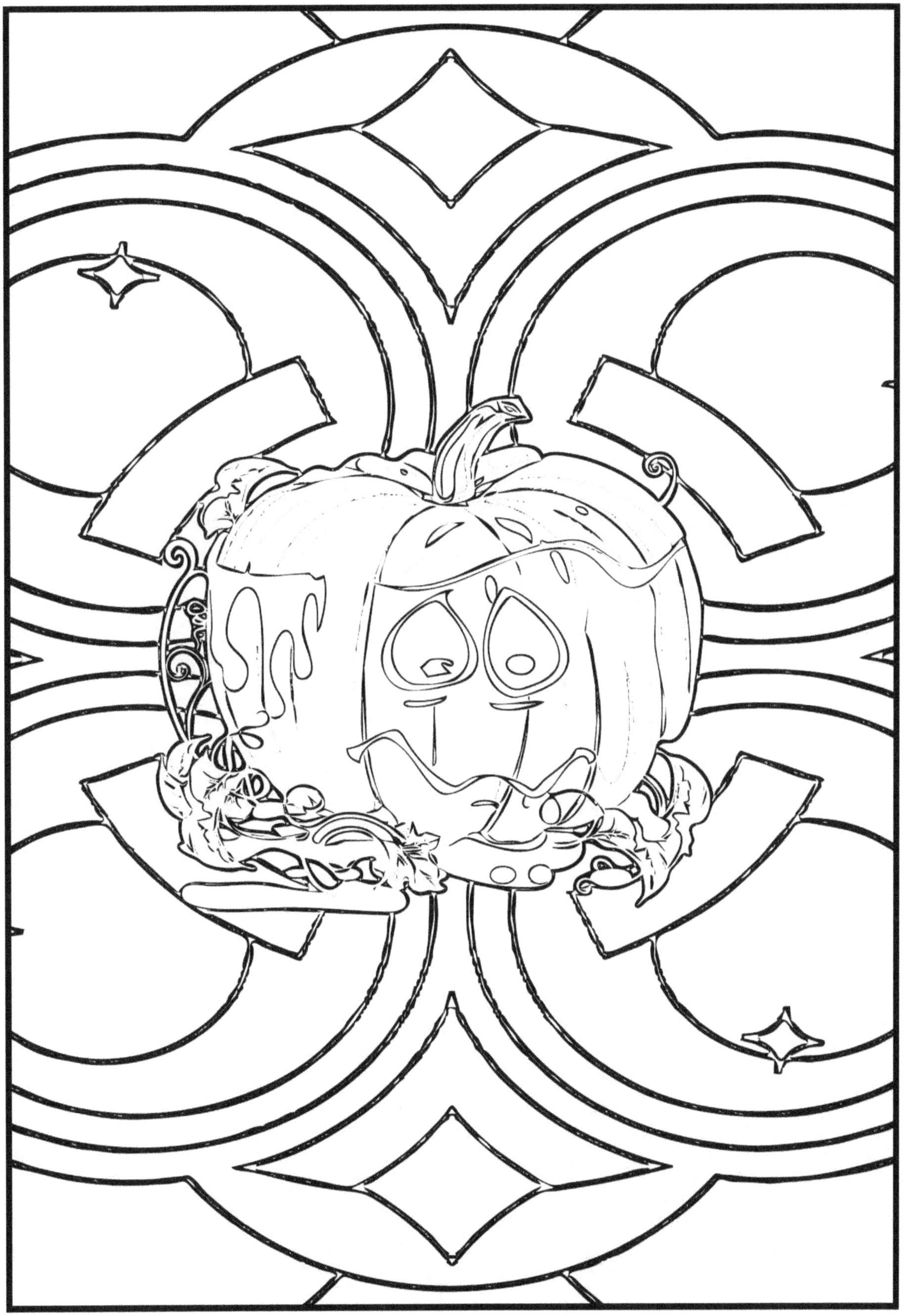

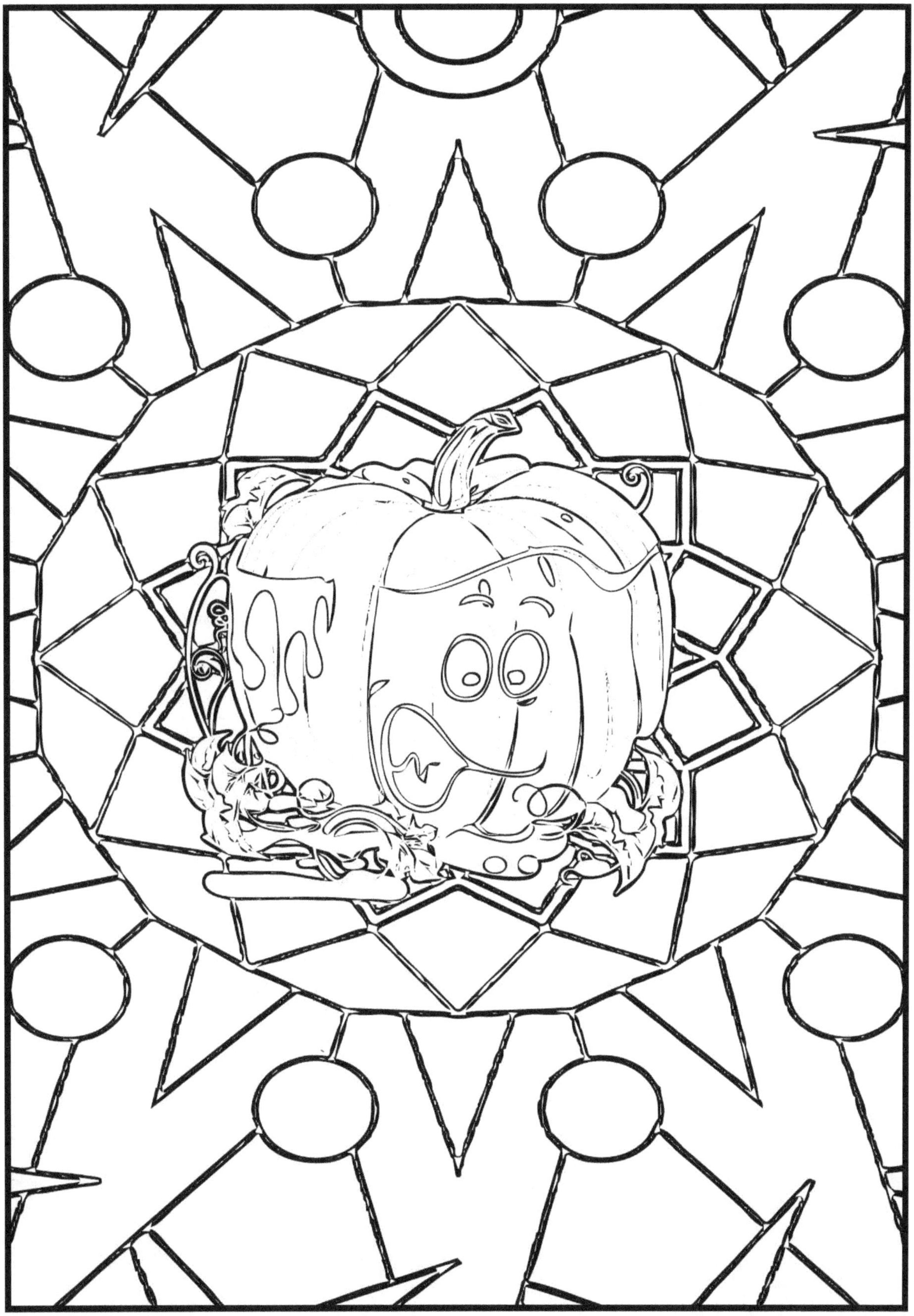

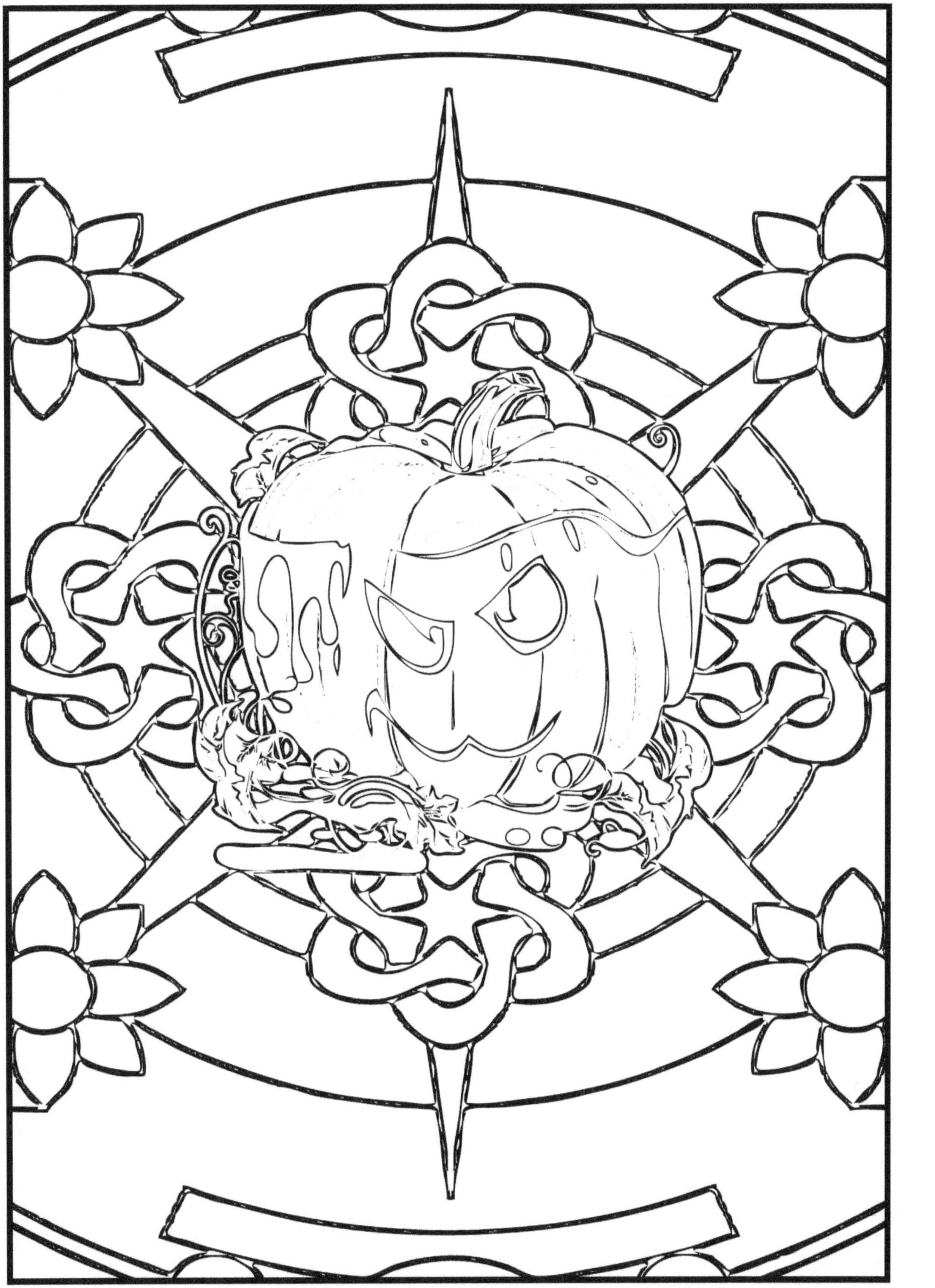

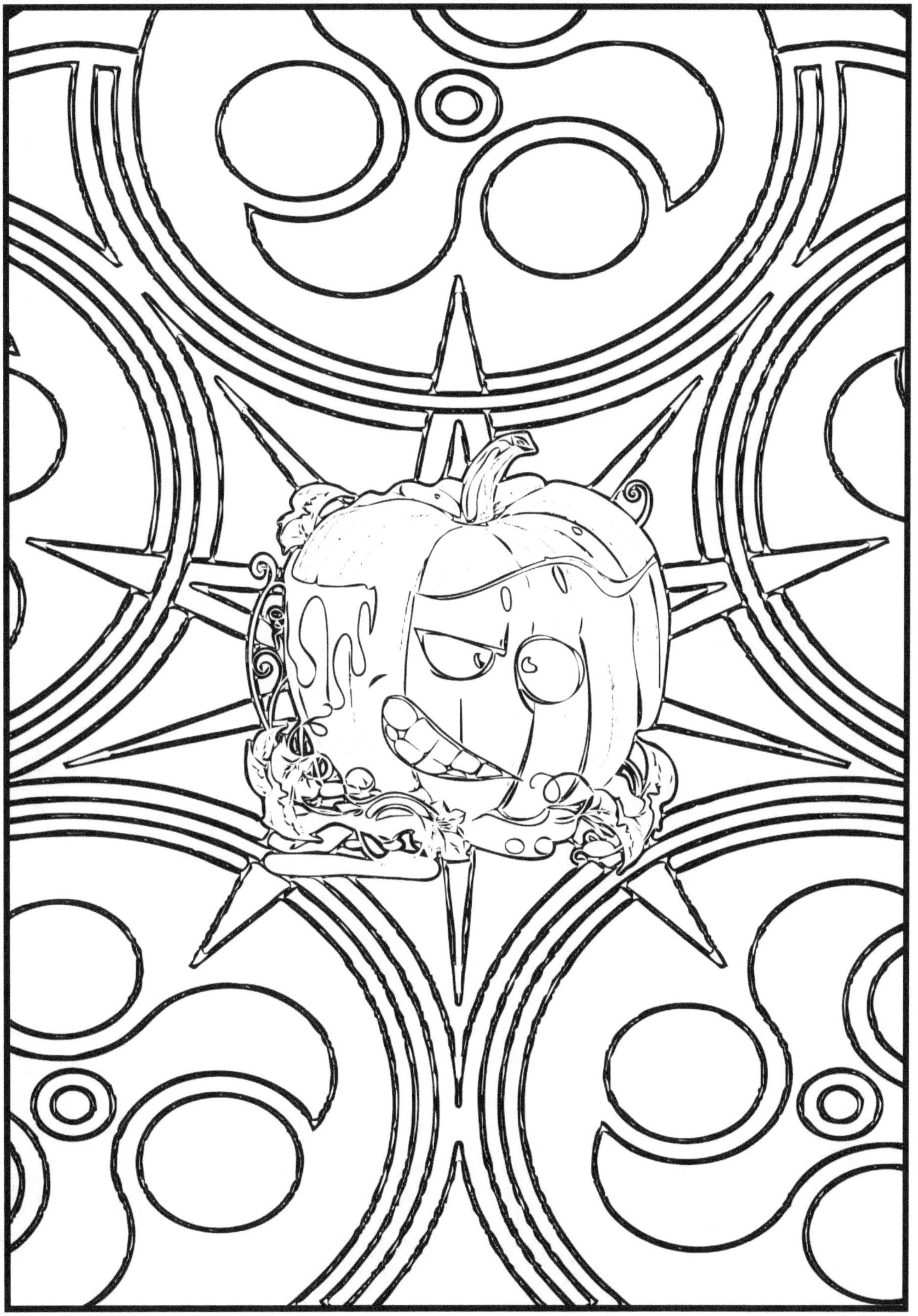

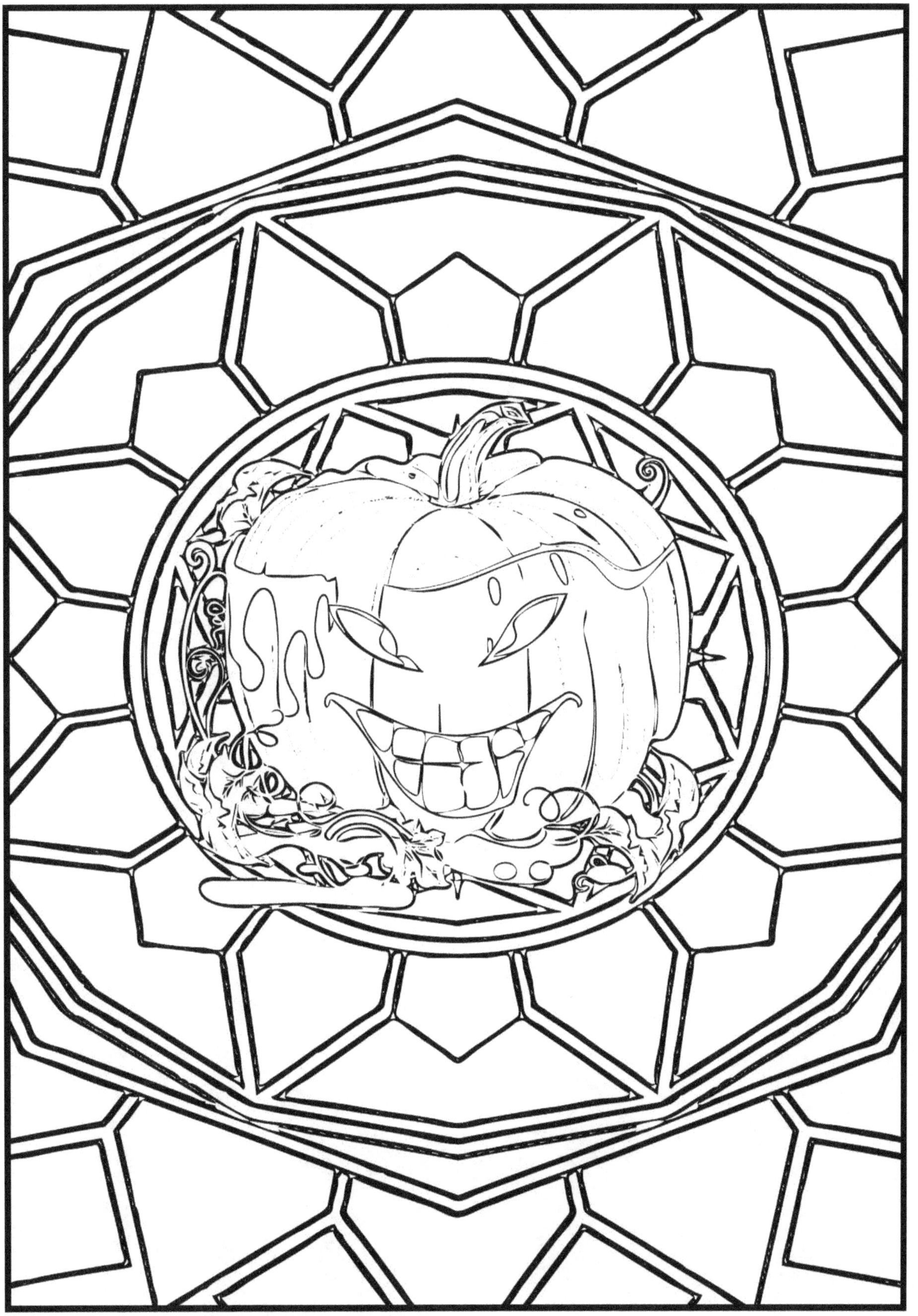

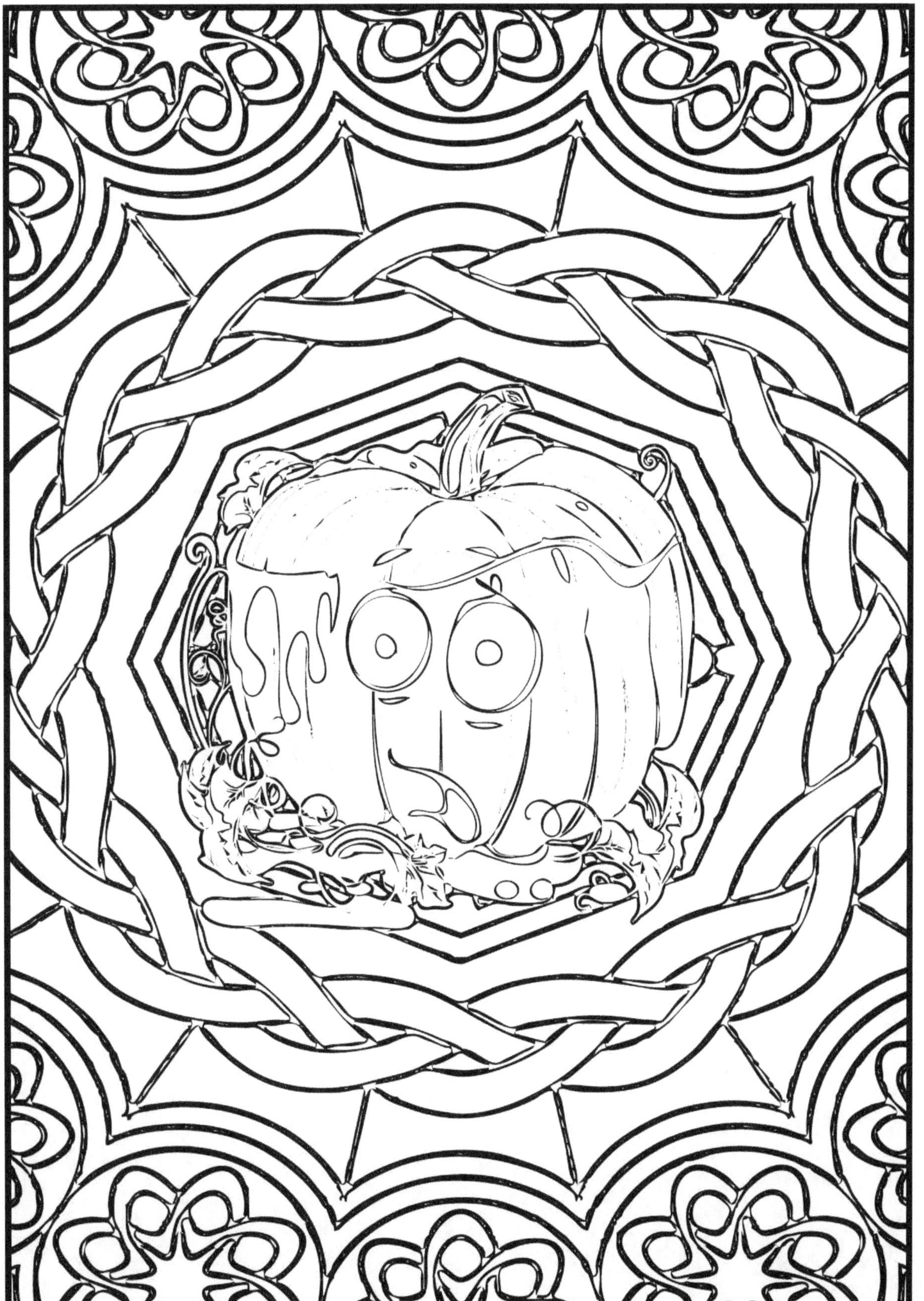

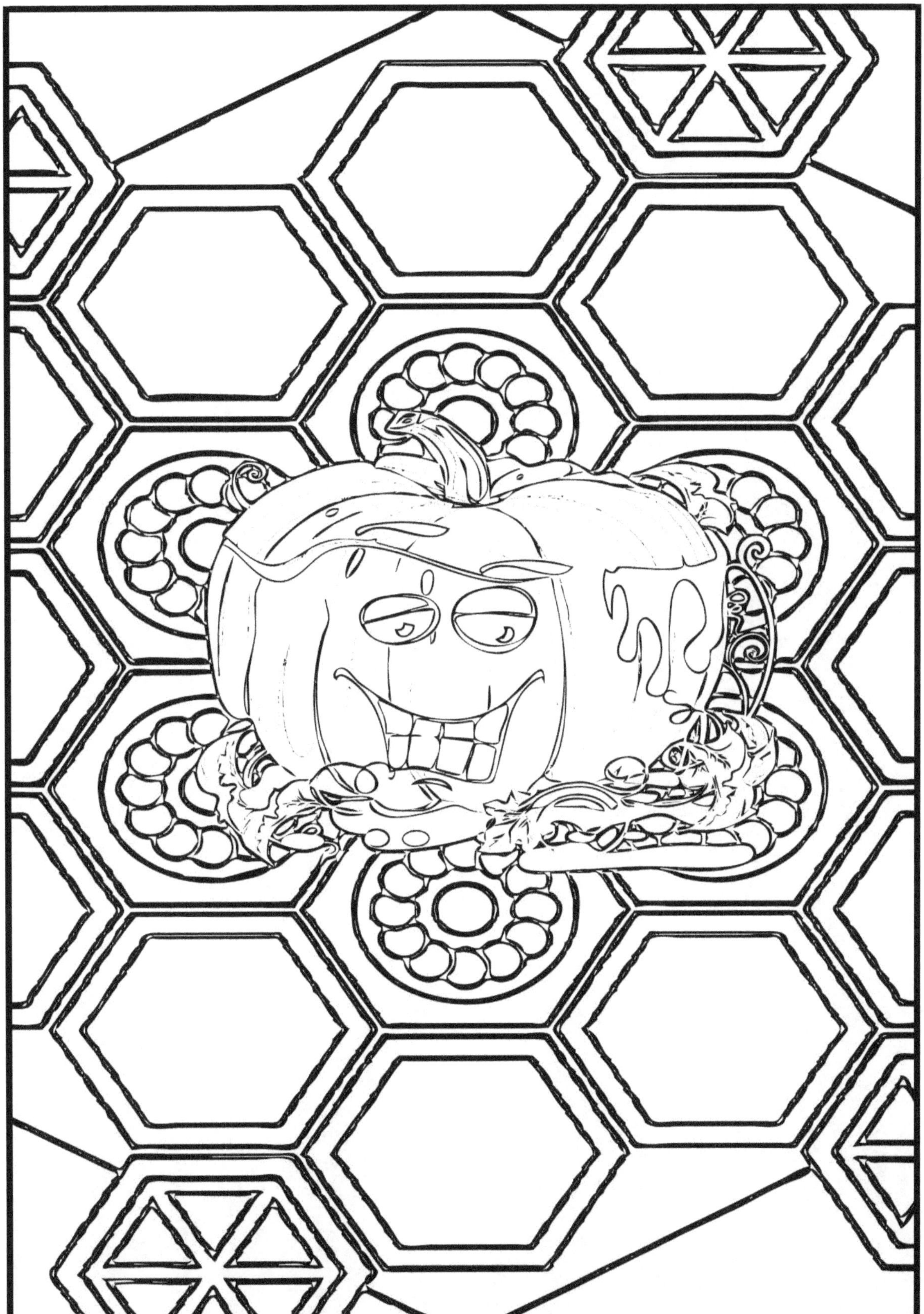

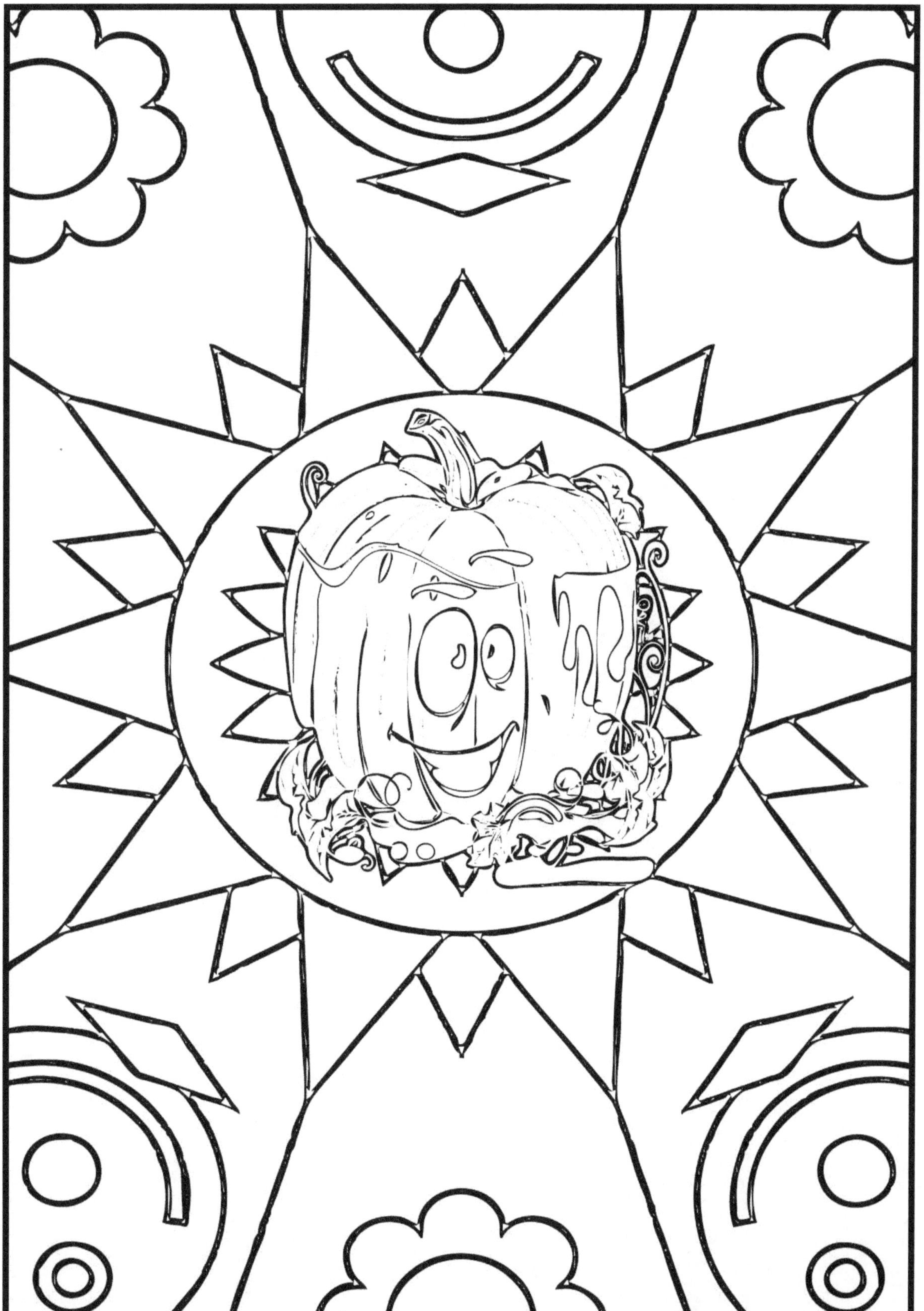

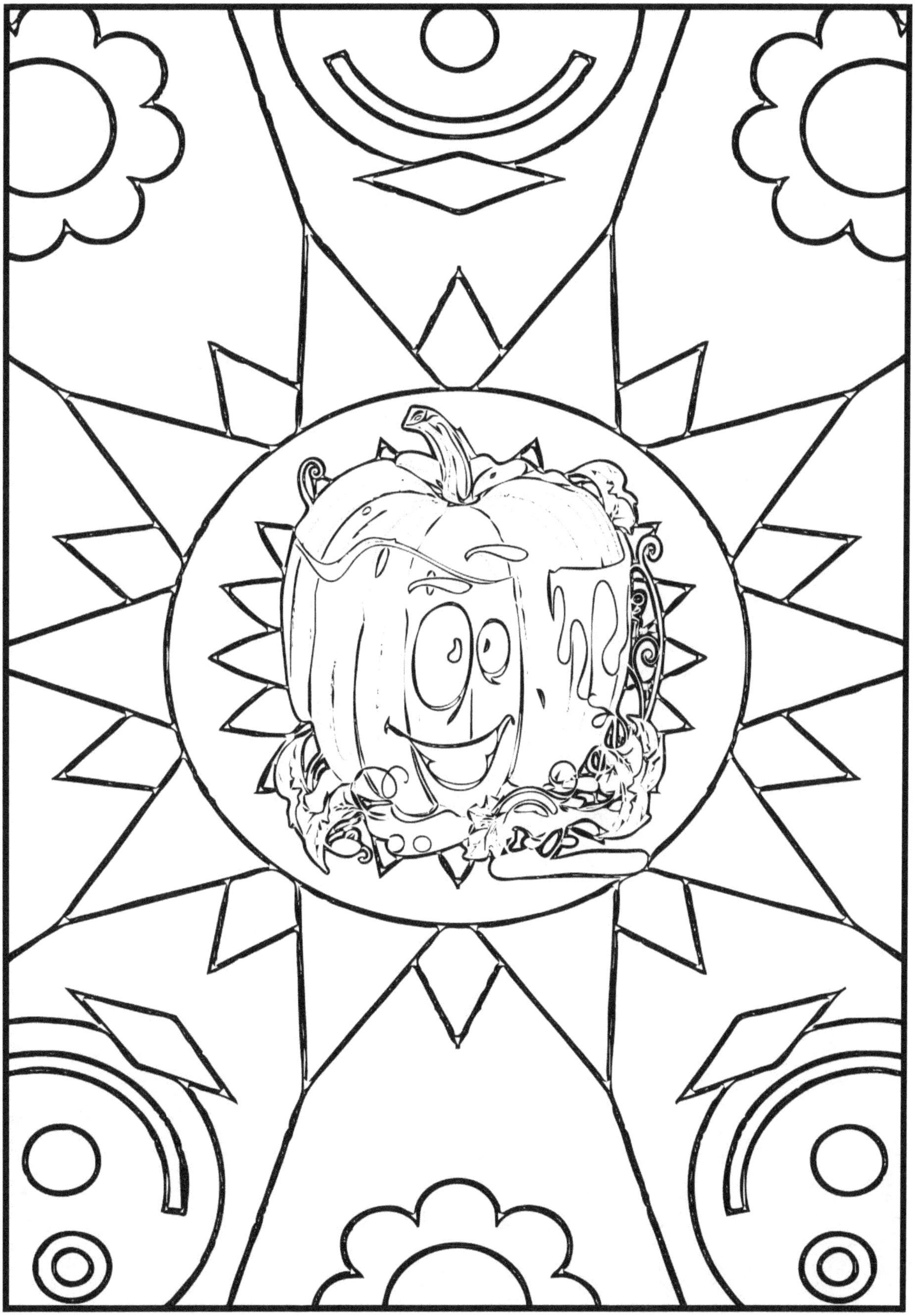

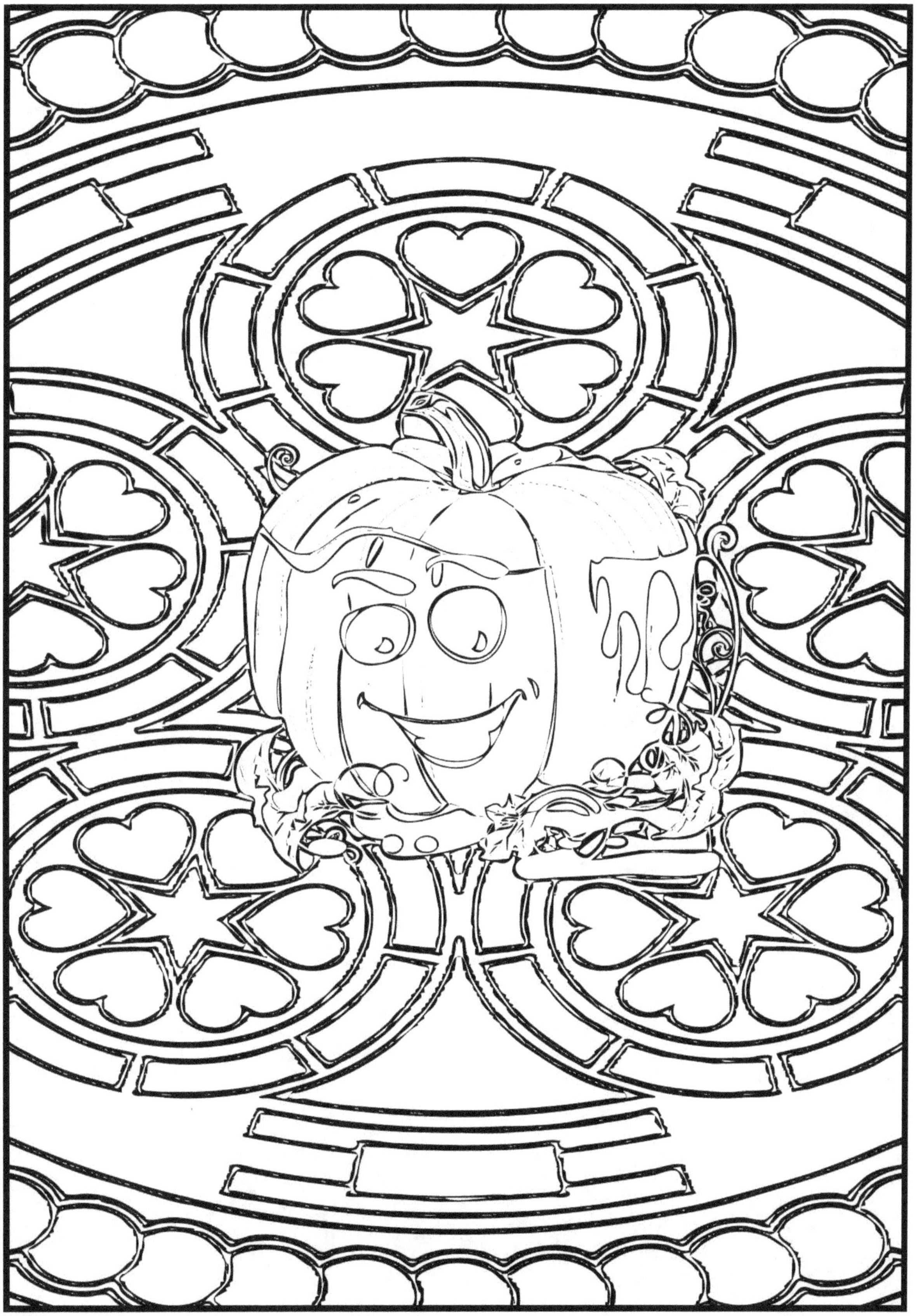

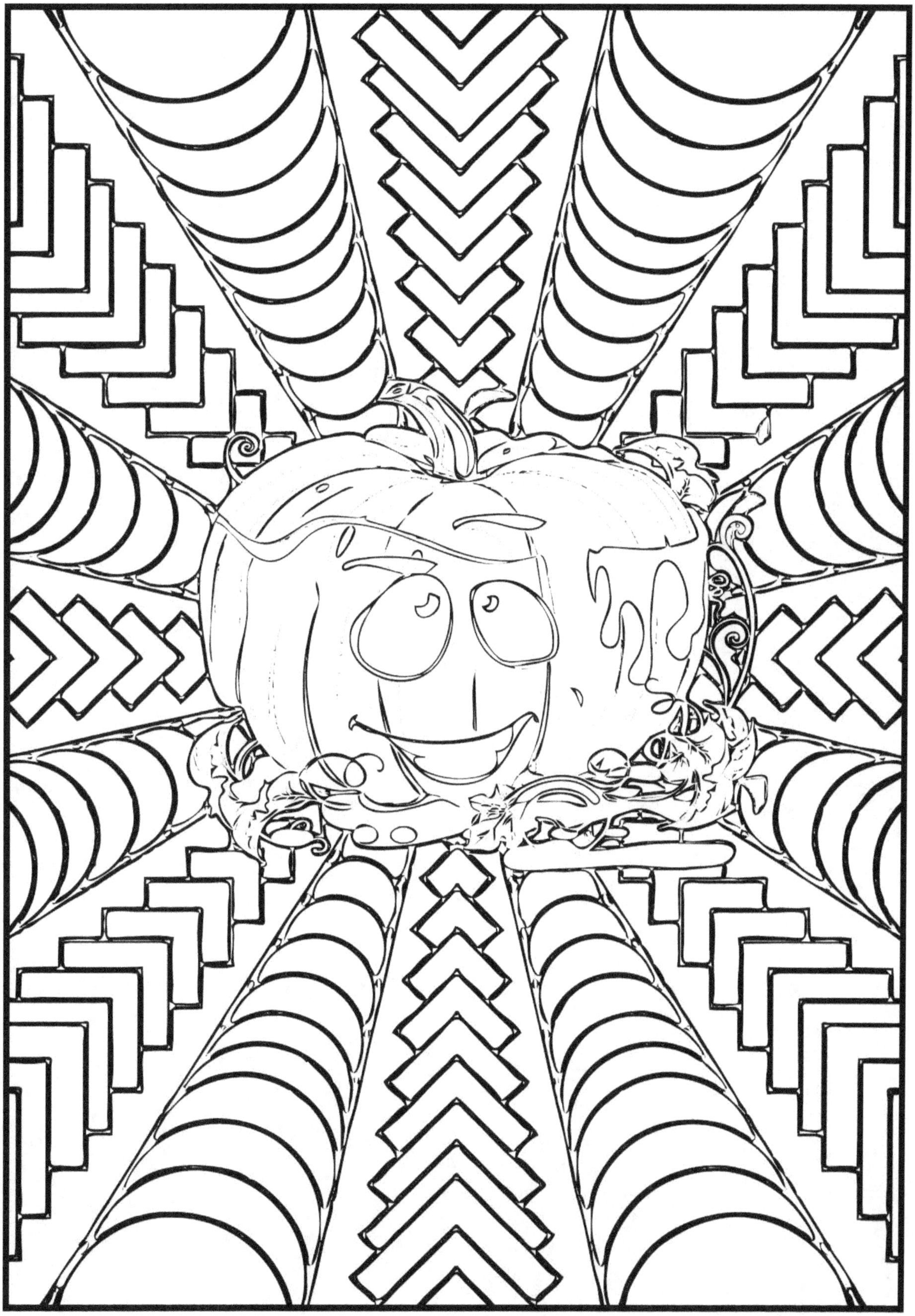

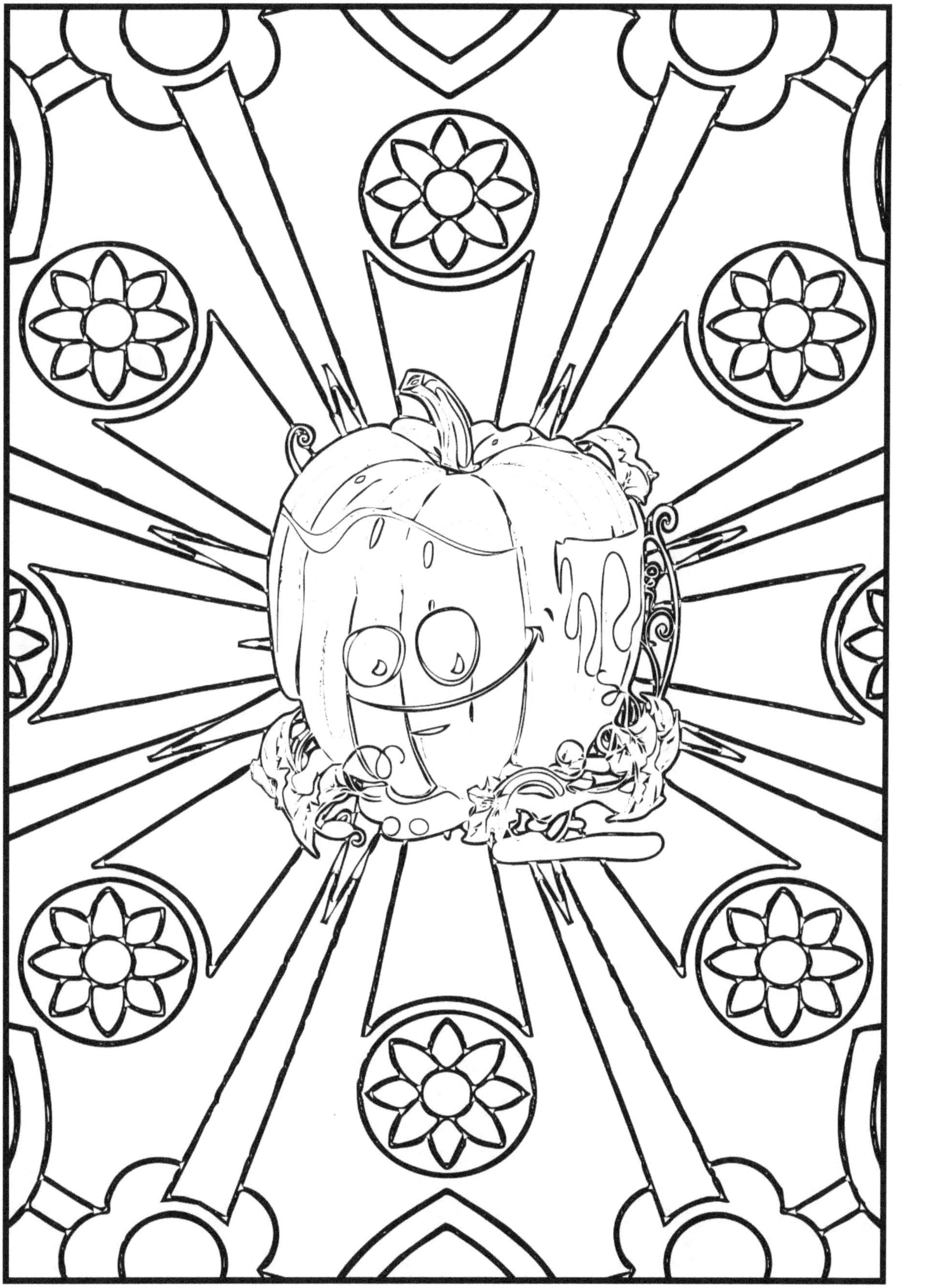

www.ingramcontent.com/pod-product-compliance
Lightning Source LLC
Chambersburg PA
CBHW080610180526
45168CB00007B/2858
* 9 7 8 1 5 1 8 6 4 9 5 5 4 *